CW00811908

SIGN LANGUAGE FOR KIDS

Tony R. Smith

A

B

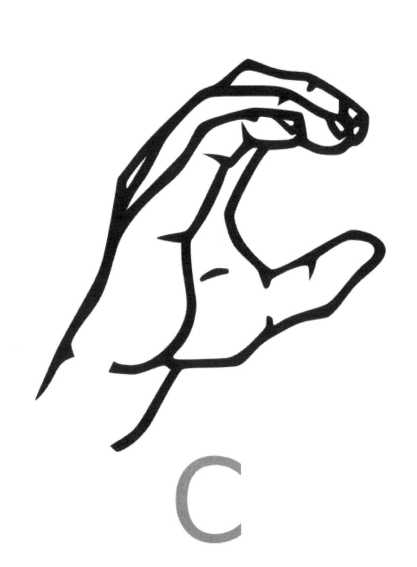

C

D

E

F

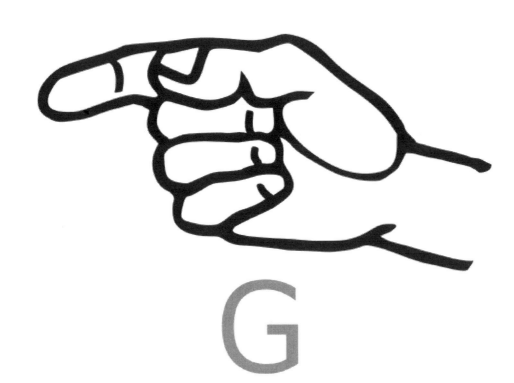

G

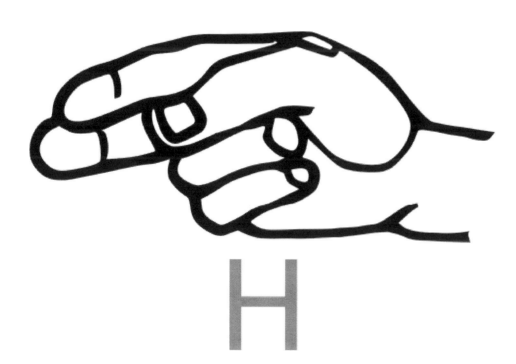

H

I

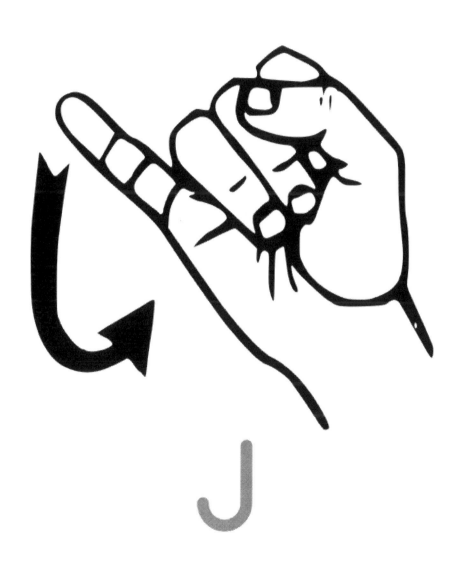

J

K

L

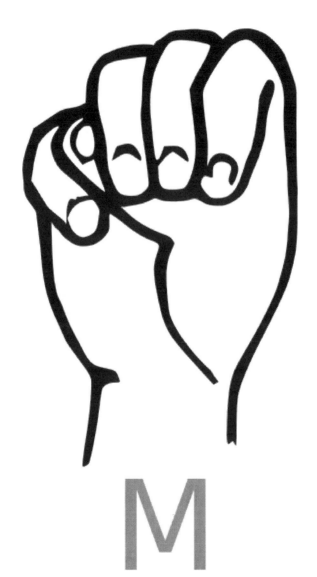

M

N

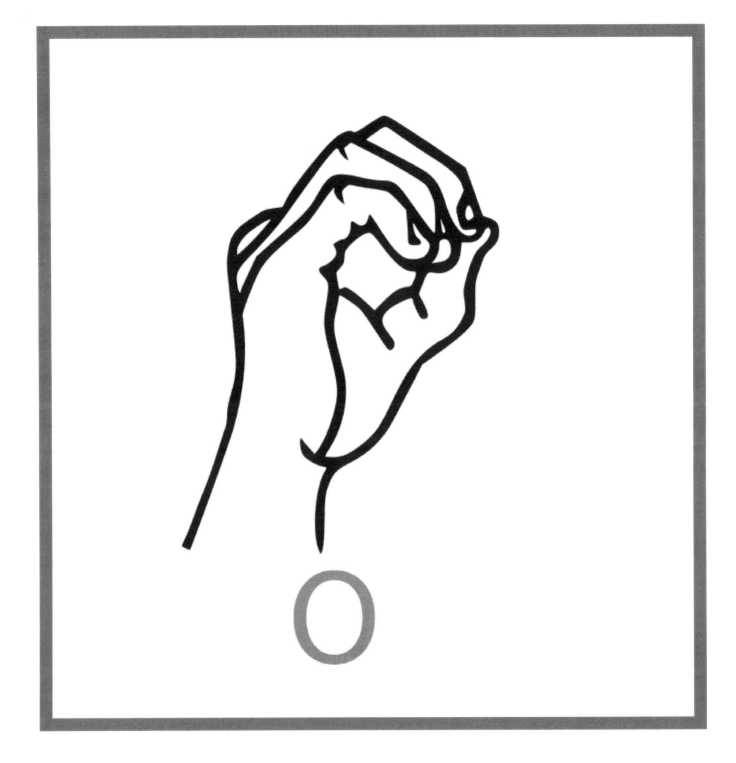

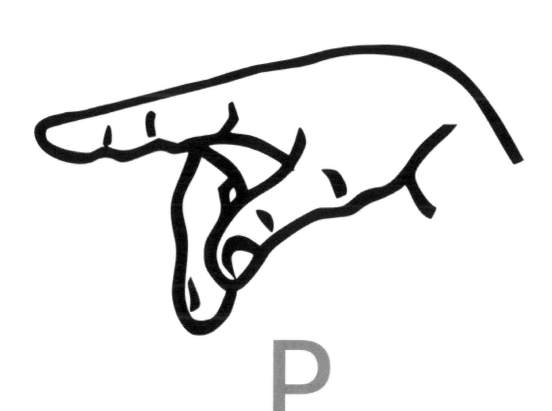

P

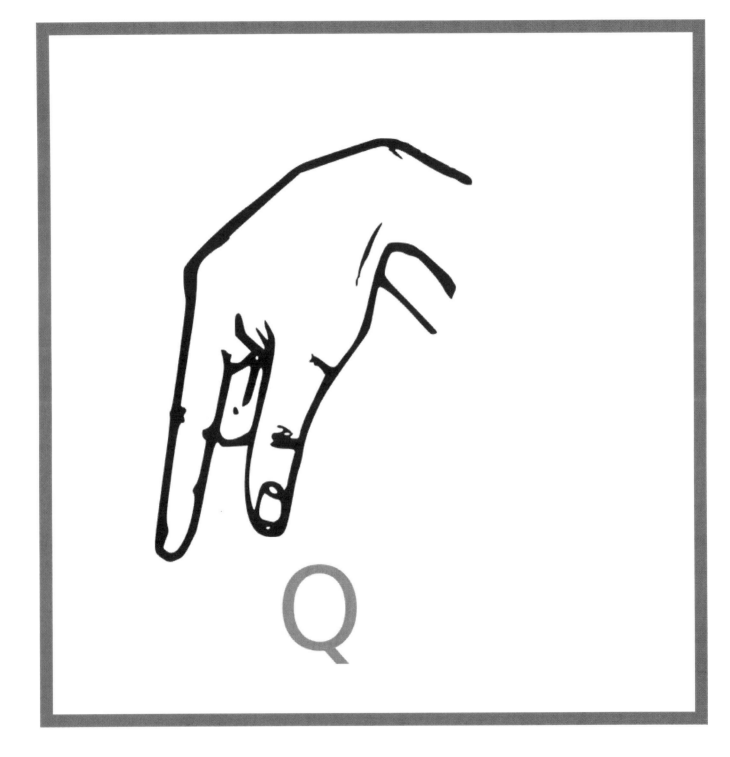

R

S

T

U

W

X

Y

Numbers

Fill in the Number

5	3			7				
6			1	9	5			
	9	8					6	
8				6				3
4			8		3			1
7				2				6
	6					2	8	
			4	1	9			5
				8			7	9

STAR HERE

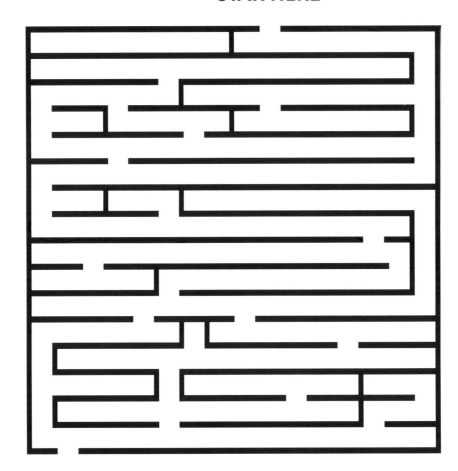

COME OUT HERE

ZERO

0

ONE

1

TWO

2

THREE

3

FOUR

4

FIVE

5

SIX

6

SEVEN

7

EIGHT

8

NINE

9

TEN

10

Emergency Room Talk

Emergency Room Talk

Admit/Enter

Ambulance

Emergency

Hemorrage/Bleed

Hospital
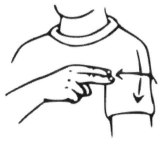

Discharge
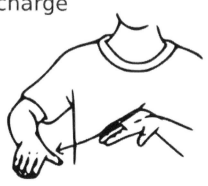

Medical Procedures

Bandage

Blood Pressure

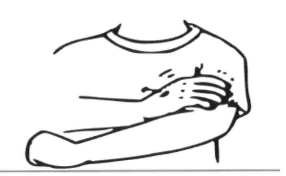

Draw Blood

Injection

Medical Procedures

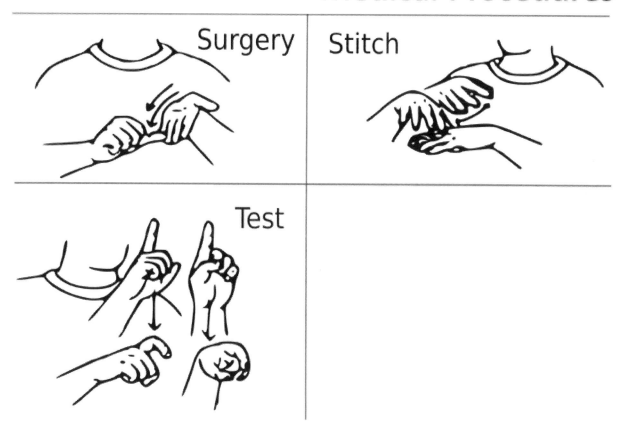

Surgery

Stitch

Test

Remedies

Bedrest/Rest

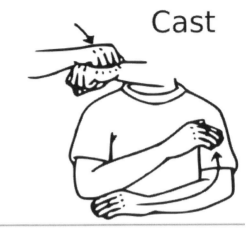

Cast

Crutches

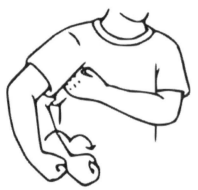

Prescription

Wheelchair

Basic Words

Find your way out

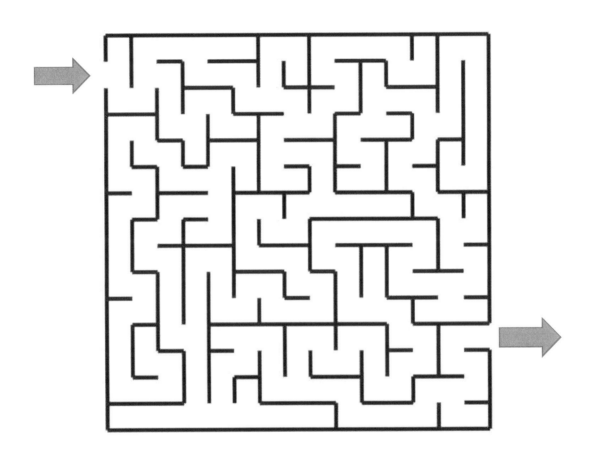

Find your way out

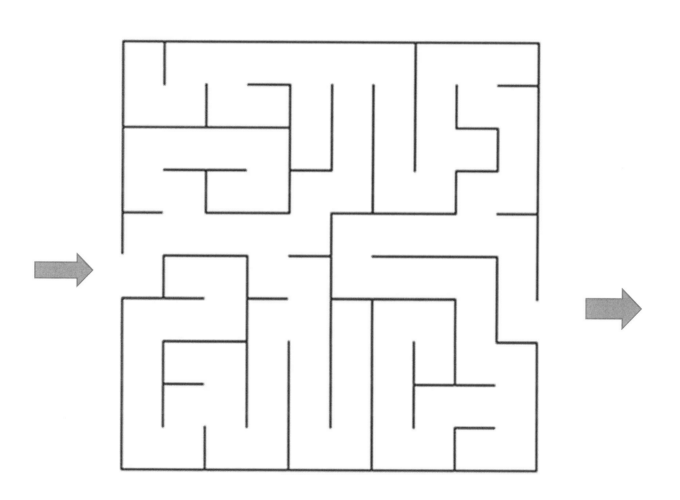

bathroom

book

goodbye

hello

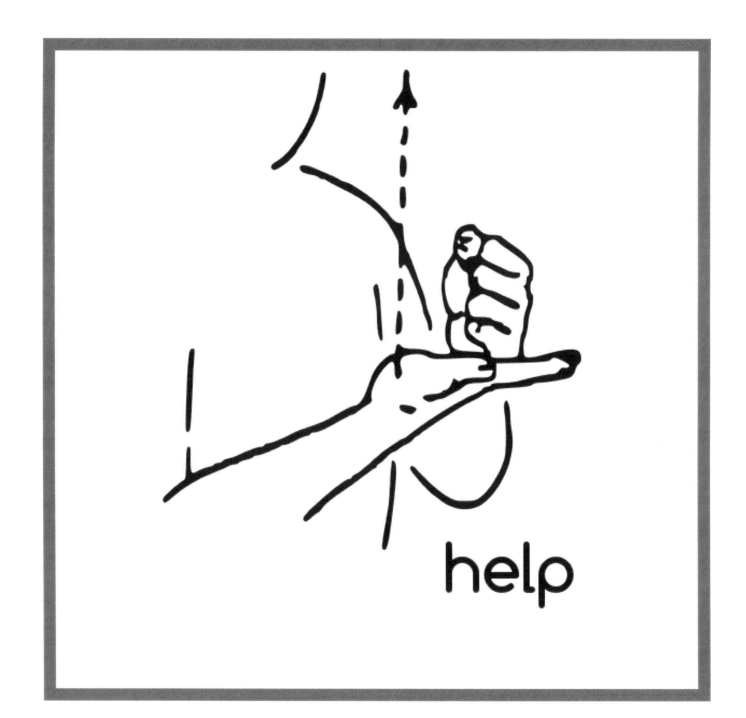

help

internet

no

please

sorry

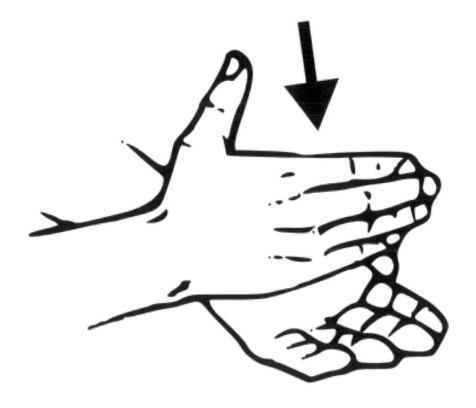

stop

thanks

thanks/good/welcome

what

when

where

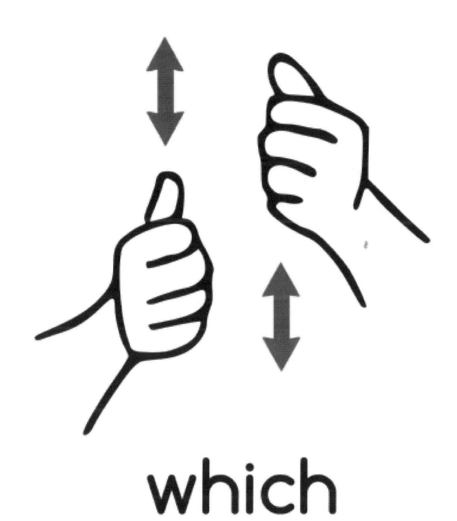

which

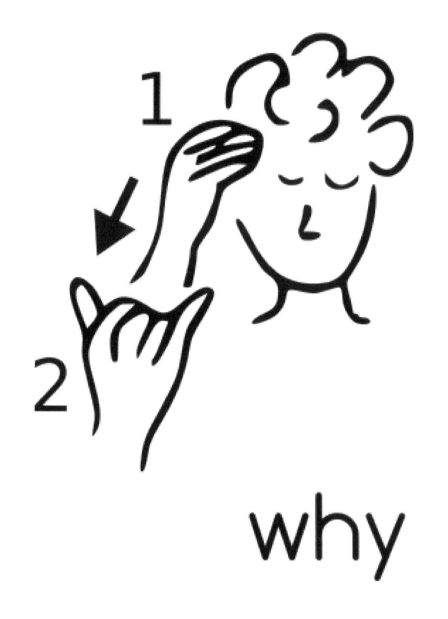

why

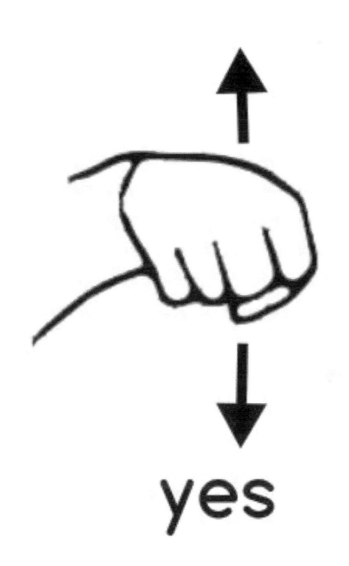

yes

Answers

5	3	4	6	7	8	9	1	2
6	7	2	1	9	5	3	4	8
1	9	8	3	4	2	5	6	7
8	5	9	7	6	1	4	2	3
4	2	6	8	5	3	7	9	1
7	1	3	9	2	4	8	5	6
9	6	1	5	3	7	2	8	4
2	8	7	4	1	9	6	3	5
3	4	5	2	8	6	1	7	9

BONUS SECTION
NAME THE ANIMAL
HAND SECTION

BONUS SECTION

NAME THE ANIMAL

_____

BONUS SECTION

NAME THE ANIMAL

_____

BONUS SECTION

NAME THE ANIMAL

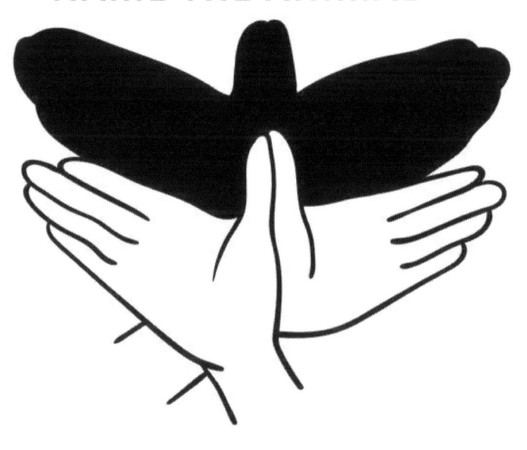

_____

BONUS SECTION

NAME THE ANIMAL

_____ _____ _____ _____ _____ _____ _____ _____ _____ _____

BONUS SECTION

NAME THE ANIMAL

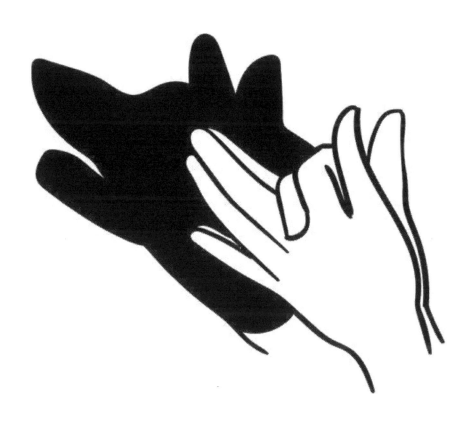

___ ___ ___ ___ ___ ___ ___ ___ ___ ___

BONUS SECTION

NAME THE ANIMAL

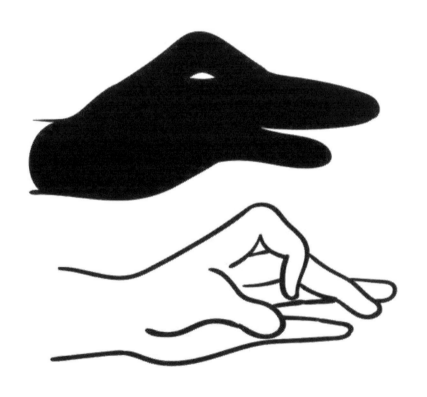

_____ _____ _____ _____ _____ _____ _____ _____ _____ _____

BONUS SECTION

NAME THE ANIMAL

___ ___ ___ ___ ___ ___ ___ ___ ___ ___

BONUS SECTION

NAME THE ANIMAL

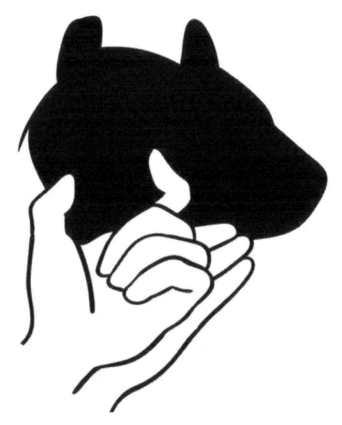

_____

BONUS SECTION

NAME THE ANIMAL

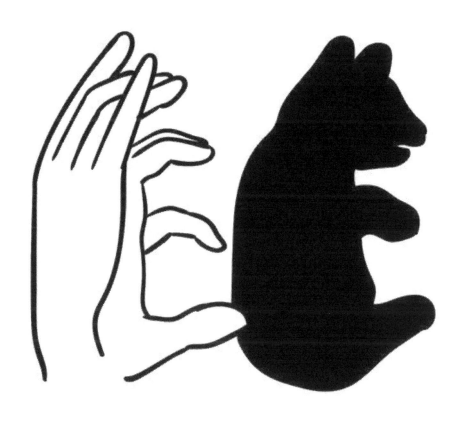

_____ _____ _____ _____ _____ _____ _____ _____ _____

BONUS SECTION

NAME THE ANIMAL

__ __ __ __ __ __ __ __ __ __ __ __

BONUS SECTION

NAME THE ANIMAL

__ __ __ __ __ __ __ __ __ __ __ __

BONUS SECTION
BODY SIGNS

Elbow Plank

Elbow Plank (Knee)

Bent Knee Side Plank

Side Plank

Side Plank Leg Lift

Basic Plank

Plank Leg Raise

Plank Arm Reach

Side Plank
Knee Tuck (1)

Side Plank
Knee Tuck (2)

Elevated Side Plank

Ball Plank

Ball Plank Reverse

Extended Plank

Reverse Plank

Jumping Jacks

Side Kick

Squatting

Push-up

Rotation

Knee Bent Push-up

Pelvic Scoop

Lunge

Chair Step Up

Wall Sit

Burpees

Donkey Kick

Abdominal Crunch

Superman

Single-Leg Bridge

Knee Crunches

Flutter Kick

Cycling Crunches

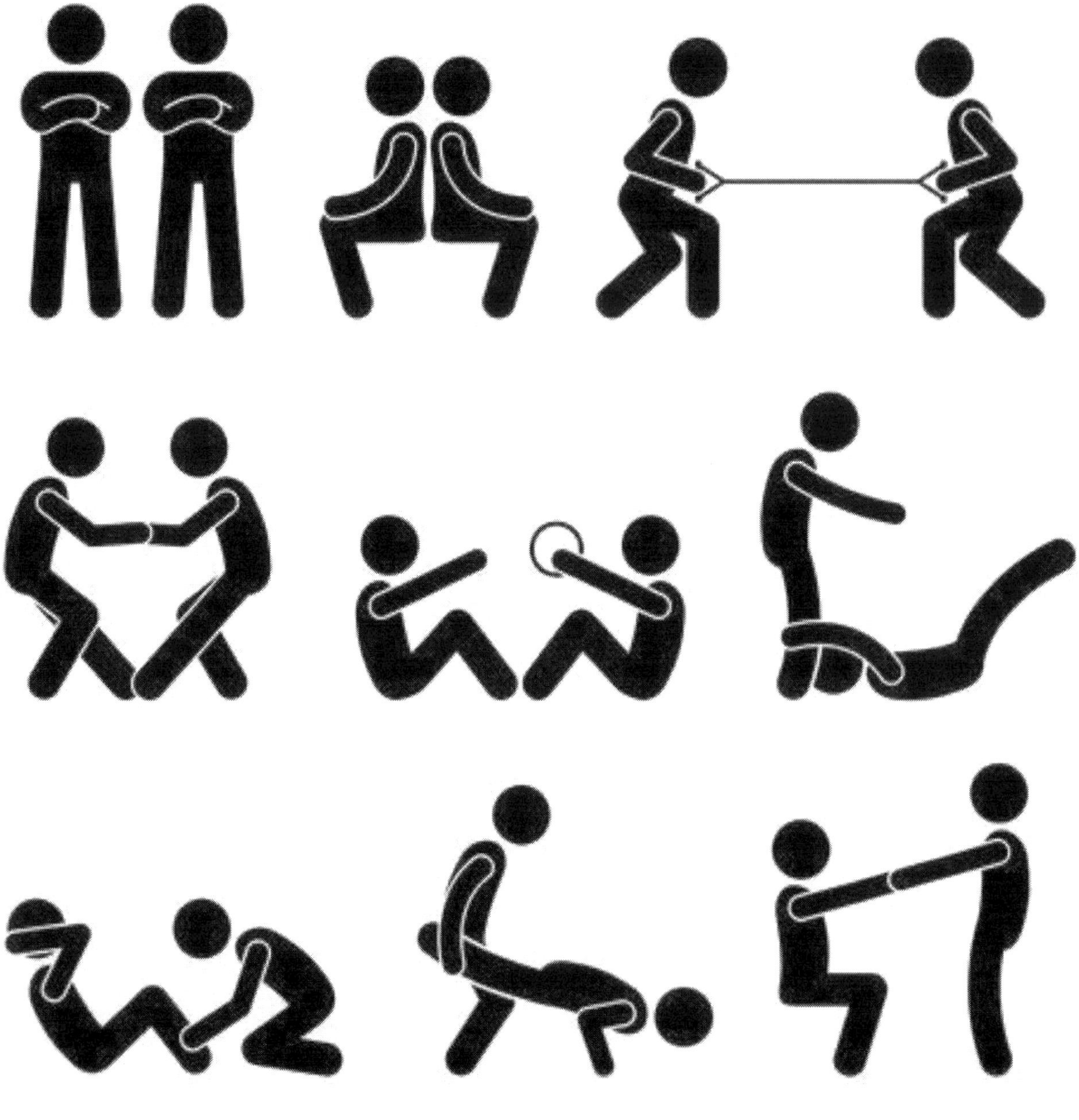

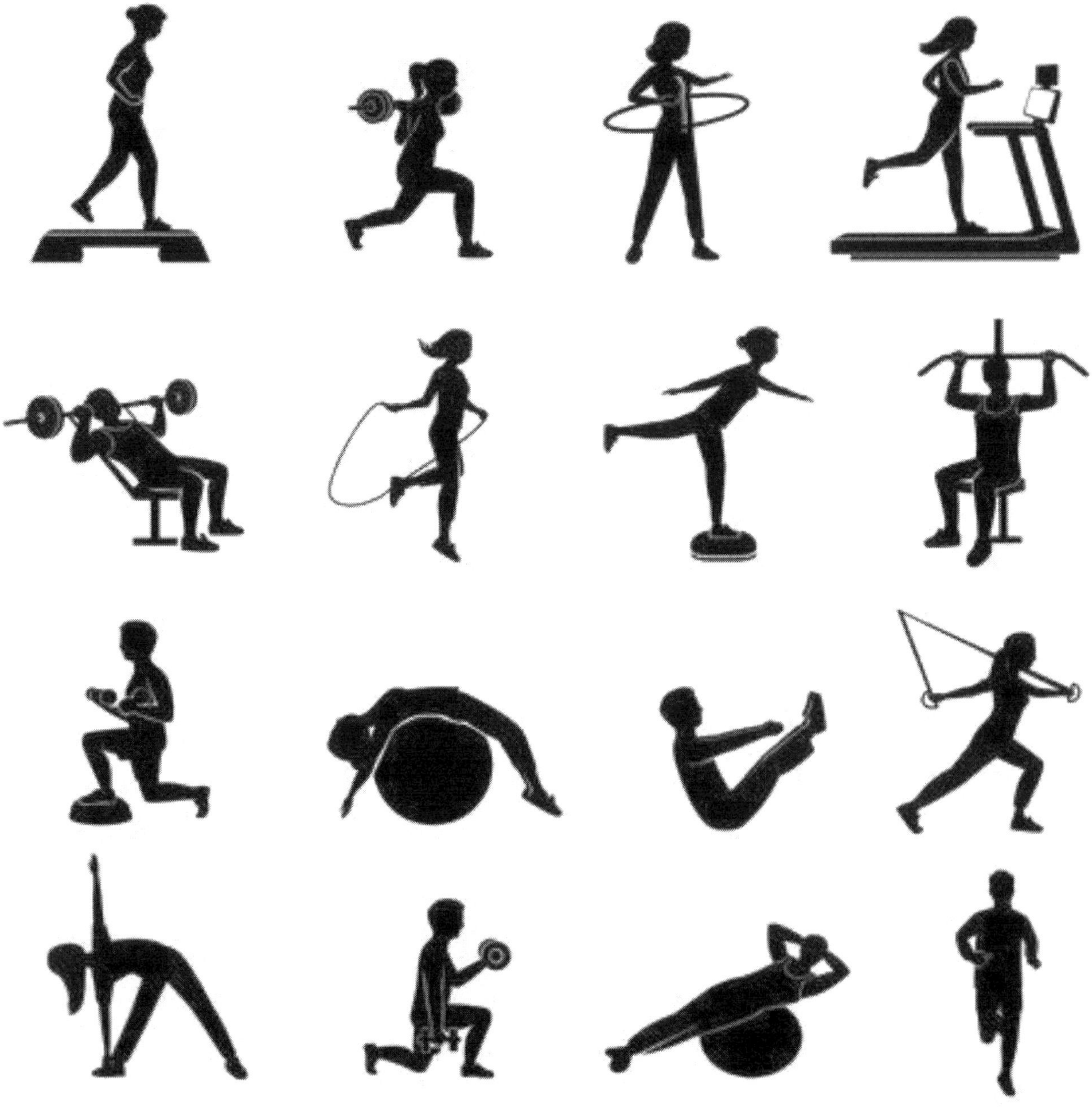

DRAW HAND SIGNS

DRAW HAND SIGNS

DRAW HAND SIGNS

DRAW HAND SIGNS

DRAW HAND SIGNS

DRAW HAND SIGNS

DRAW HAND SIGNS

DRAW HAND SIGNS

DRAW HAND SIGNS

Printed in Great Britain
by Amazon